Tales of Travelers

Three European Fables

Yvonne Coppard

Illustrated by Eva Sykorova-Pekarkova

Rigby®

A Harcourt Achieve Imprint

www.Rigby.com
1-800-531-5015

Literacy by Design Leveled Readers: *Tales of Travelers: Three European Fables*

ISBN-13:   978-1-4189-3668-5
ISBN-10:   1-4189-3668-6

Printed in China
3 4 5 6 7 8 985 14 13 12 11 10 09 08

Contents

The Peddler of Swaffham

Long ago, in a place called Swaffham, in the country of England, there lived a peddler who traveled around selling small but useful things.

"I have cooking pots, ribbons, and string," he would call out. "Come and buy them!"

But the people were very poor, and they could not afford to buy these things, however useful they might be.

"What can we do?" cried his wife. "We don't have enough money to buy food, and so we'll starve."

"We will not starve," said the peddler, trying to comfort his wife. But truthfully, he was worried, too.

That night, the peddler had a strange dream. He saw a huge bridge in London, with many people and horses crossing it. The bridge was so big that there were stores lining both sides!

In his dream, a voice said, "Go to London Bridge and stay. You will hear something that will change your life in a wonderful way."

The peddler told his wife about the dream and asked her if he should go.

The peddler's wife laughed and said, "Don't be foolish. Dreams will not put bread on the table."

"Yes, you're right," said the peddler sadly.

The next night, and the night after that, the peddler had the dream again.

"Go to London Bridge and stay," said the voice. "You will hear something that will change your life in a wonderful way."

The peddler said to his wife, "I have to go to London."

His wife began to cry. "You fool!" she said. "London is a dangerous city. You will be robbed."

The peddler said, "Who will rob me when I have nothing? Listen, dear, I must go. Please, kiss me goodbye and try to understand."

The peddler's wife thought he was foolish, but she loved him, and so she kissed him goodbye.

"Go, if you must," she said. "I will wait for you every day, so please think of me, and hurry home."

She was sad as she watched him go.

It was a long way to London. The peddler walked all day on winding roads where he came across other travelers and he told them about his strange dream. Every single one of them laughed out loud, but some gave him food and a little money.

"What a foolish man," they said, feeling sorry for him.

The peddler traveled on, and at night, he slept under bushes. He made a pillow from grass and a blanket from leaves. Animals from the fields wandered up to him and sniffed him, wondering why he was there.

"They would laugh too, if they knew," thought the peddler, but still he traveled on.

At last the peddler came to London and found his way to London Bridge. Everywhere he looked, there were people, horses, and carts, just like his dream. A large number of shops lined both sides of the bridge.

He found a quiet spot outside the baker's shop and waited. He waited all day, and then he curled up in a quiet corner of the bridge to sleep.

The next morning, he stood again in the same spot. Night came, and he slept in the same corner. This went on for three days.

The peddler was very sad. "I must go home," he said to himself, "for I am indeed a fool."

The peddler had one small coin left in his pocket, so he went into the baker's shop to buy some bread.

"I have been watching you," said the baker. "Why do you stand out there all alone?"

The peddler told the baker about his dream, and the baker laughed.

"You fool!" he said. "You came all this way for nothing. Why, I myself had a strange dream not so long ago, but I took no notice for I am not such a fool."

"What was your dream?" asked the peddler.

"I dreamed about a place called Swaffham," laughed the baker. "I have never heard of it, but there I saw a peddler's cottage with an apple tree behind it. A voice told me that under the apple tree, there was a chest full of gold."

Trembling, the peddler left the baker's shop. "I must go home as fast as I can," he said.

"I thought you would never come home!" said the peddler's wife when she saw her husband.

The peddler was very happy to see her, but he wanted to check the baker's dream right away. The peddler grabbed his shovel and started to dig.

"Have you gone crazy?" asked his wife. "Why are you digging under the tree?"

"My dream was right. I did hear something wonderful," said the peddler. Sure enough, he lifted out a heavy chest, and once he opened it, he saw that it was full of gold.

The peddler and his wife danced around the tree. "We will never be hungry again!" they shouted joyfully.

And they never were.

❦ Moral ❦

*Don't let other people stop
you from following
your dreams if you think it's
the right thing to do.*

17

A Good Teacher

There was once a rich farmer who lived near the mountains of Bugeci, in Romania, a country of beautiful forests. The farmer had everything money could buy. He owned a big stretch of land and loved his work on the farm. He had one son, whom he loved very much.

The son was kind, generous, and hard-working, and the farmer was proud of his son. Everybody who met the son liked him right away.

The farmer wanted to teach his son how to solve problems on his own, however.

One time, he gave his son a sack with a hole in it to use to carry potatoes. Then the farmer gave his son a knife that wasn't sharp enough to cut vegetables. Another time, he hid the boy's coat.

But every time the farmer gave his son a problem, someone helped the boy solve it. The milkmaid sewed his sack, the woodcutter sharpened his knife, and the shepherd's mother found him another coat.

"Thank you so much," said the son each time.

"We are glad to help you," everyone said. However, the son still had no idea how to deal with problems by himself.

One day the farmer called his son to him. "I want you to go deep into the forest," he said. "The trees that grow right in the center are the best. Please chop down three tall, straight trees and bring them back. We will use them to build a new fence."

"Yes, Father," said the son happily. "I will need to take a cart with me."

"Here you are," said his father, pointing to a very old cart with wooden wheels.

"Father, I don't think this cart is very good," said his son. "Look at how wobbly it is. Can I take one of the new carts?"

"No," said the farmer. "I am sorry, son, but I need all the other carts on the farm. This is the one you must take. Just remember, if you get into any kind of trouble, necessity will show you what you should do."

The boy set off for the forest and soon found the place where the straight, tall trees grew. He collected enough wood to make a very nice fence. Then he loaded up the cart and set off for home.

Suddenly, a wheel on his cart fell off.

"What shall I do now?" thought the farmer's son. "I can't push a cart with one wheel."

Then he remembered what his father had told him. "Necessity will help me," he said cheerfully.

But where was Necessity? The farmer's son had not seen a single person all day.

"Necessity!" he called out.

His voice drifted into the trees, but there was no answer.

The farmer's son called again, "Necessity, where are you? I need help!"

His voice drifted across the forest floor, but still nobody showed up to help him.

"Perhaps Necessity's busy chopping wood, or swimming in the river," thought the farmer's son, "and that's why she can't hear me."

He walked around the forest for a long time, calling and searching for Necessity, but there was nobody in the forest but him.

"My father was wrong," thought the boy. "There is nobody here to help me, which means that I will have to work out what to do for myself."

He sat down and thought. He thought for a long time. Then he got up, chopped some wood and sawed it into the shape he wanted. He made the wood into a new wheel and fixed his cart.

It was getting dark, and back at the farm, the farmer was worried. "I should not have sent my son off on his own," he thought sadly. "He is probably in trouble, and he doesn't know what to do."

Then the farmer heard singing. He turned around to see his son making his way out of the forest, pushing a cart piled high with wood.

"There you are!" cried the farmer happily.

"I'm sorry if you were worried, Father," said the boy. "The cart broke, and I couldn't find Necessity, so I had to fix it all by myself."

Then the farmer knew that his son would be able to take care of himself if he had a problem.

"My son," he said, "you did indeed find Necessity."

❧ Moral ❧
Look at what skills you have instead of always depending on others.

Stone Soup

Long ago, a traveler made a journey through Portugal. He walked along Portugal's coast, and looked out over the huge Atlantic Ocean. He traveled on until he reached a small town.

The stranger walked through the town, carrying a sack across his shoulder.

"Good day," he said. "I am just passing through. I'm cold and hungry. Do you have anything to share with me?"

Everyone the stranger asked for help said the same thing. "We are hungry, too, and we have nothing to spare."

The weather had been bad that year, and so the people in the village had not been able to grow much food. Besides, this man was a stranger. People wondered why he was there, in this ordinary town, for they did not get many visitors.

The stranger walked on. When
he reached the town square, he
stopped. From his sack, he took
out some firewood and made a fire.
Then he took out a pot, poured
water from the town well into it,
and set it over the fire. He took a
large stone from his sack, put it into
the water, and then sat down to
wait for the water to get hot.

A woman passed by. "Stranger, what do you have in there?" she asked.

"Stone soup," said the stranger.

"What is that?" asked the woman.

"You don't know about stone soup?" asked the stranger, looking very surprised. "Madam, I have traveled the world, and I can tell you that I have never tasted better soup than this."

The woman peered into the pot. "It looks like a stone in some water," she said.

The stranger sighed. "To be honest, it does need an onion," he said.

The woman was curious about this wonderful soup. "I have an onion," she said. "Will you share your soup?"

"Yes, I will," said the stranger, with a smile.

The woman brought an onion to add to the soup and sat down with the stranger to wait.

A man came along. "What are you doing?" he asked.

"The stranger and I are waiting for our stone soup to cook," the woman replied. "It is the best soup in the world."

"Stone soup?" The man looked into the pot and sniffed. "It doesn't look like much."

"Well, it really needs some carrots," the stranger said with a sigh.

The man said, "If I give you carrots, will you share your soup with me?"

"Of course," said the stranger, with a smile.

The man ran home and returned soon after, his arms full of juicy carrots, freshly picked from his garden. The stranger looked at them happily and added them to the soup. Then they all sat together to wait.

The butcher came by, and the man told him about the wonderful stone soup.

The butcher peered into the pot.

"It doesn't look like much," he said.

"My stone soup is famous," said the stranger. "All it needs is meat to be at its best."

"I will bring you some," said the butcher, "if I can share this soup."

"There is plenty to share," said the stranger.

The butcher brought meat and waited with the group.

More people came to watch the stranger as he stirred his soup.

"The stranger is making stone soup," they were told. "It is the best soup in the world."

More people came.

"It would taste even better with some potatoes," the stranger said to a farmer.

"We just need some salt," he said to the baker, and he told the town's school teacher that a turnip would finish the soup.

And so it went on. Everyone who came put something into the pot. Then they waited, for they all wanted a share of the best soup in the world. The traveler smiled and kept on stirring.

At last, he stirred the soup for the last time. "Our stone soup is ready," he declared, with a wave of his hand.

By now, the group gathered around the pot had turned into a party. One person ran for bowls, another for spoons, and another for bread. The stranger took a big spoon from his sack and began to serve the soup.

Everyone agreed this was the best soup they had ever tasted. They sat around the little fire and ate together, and talked and sang songs until late into the night.

In the morning, the stranger took his pot and traveled on, but he left his stone for the people to use again. Whenever times were hard, they made stone soup by sharing whatever they had. Everyone agreed it truly was the best soup in the world.

🌿 Moral 🌿
*It is always good
to share, however
little you have.*